Dear Christian

A Contemporary Christian Study Guide

Lois Ibiene Tarikabor

Dear Christian
Copyright © 2023 by Lois Ibiene Tarikabor

All rights reserved. No part of this publication may be reproduced, distributed, or transmitted in any form or by any means, including photocopying, recording, or other electronic or mechanical methods, without the prior written permission of the author, except in the case of brief quotations embodied in critical reviews and certain other non-commercial uses permitted by copyright law.

Tellwell Talent
www.tellwell.ca

ISBN
978-0-2288-9373-8 (Paperback)
978-0-2288-9374-5 (eBook)

DEDICATION

I want to dedicate this book to the Holy Spirit for the guidance and directives throughout the process. To my parents [Mr Otonye and Mrs Abiye Tarikabor], who ensured that I had a strong foundation as a Christian child. To my father in the Lord, David Ibiyeomie, whom I have listened to ever since my teenage years, who made sure the foundation my parents laid found its root and bore deep into the rock of Jesus. To a very revered mentor, Apostle Joshua Selman, whose teaching ministry of the word changed and radicalized my Christianity into one of submissiveness to the heart of the father and daily total surrender to his will; To myself for yielding, writing as the spirit led, taking time out to bask in his presence to get more insight. Finally, to my immediate family members because family is forever. [Valentine, Sharon, and Kennedy Tarikabor] I value each one of you in your unique ways.

INTRODUCTION

Dear Christian, these letters I write to you concerning your faith in tandem with society are a compilation of my regular thoughts on the same subject matter for over a year. As the world evolves, there is a greater need to stick with Jesus and make Christ seen and known in every facet of our lives. Society has found extremely creative ways of leaving Jesus outside the door of its evolution. However, we are not ignorant; thus, this material exists.

In it, you would find letters that explain some deep scriptural insights, and you will find relatable letters to your situation, you will find letters that are just vulnerable in themselves written to connect to your heart, you will find letters that address the condemnation you've carried within from society inclusive of church hurts. Summarily, you will find letters in their entirety that aim to make you a better Christian, chasing after the heart of the Father and wanting to be transformed into his image and likeness.

1ST LETTER
The consciousness of the Presence of God

Dear Christian,

The first undeniable thing you must know is that "God has put his signature on earth." What do I mean? Everything about creation speaks about his divinity. How does photosynthesis happen? Day and night? Sleeping and waking up? Breathing? Life and death? It cannot be explained in its entirety logically.

Psalm 24:1: "The earth is the LORD's, and everything in it. The world & all its people belong to him." Thus, as God created humans, he formed Adam from his creation (earth) & breathed into him. Further putting his signature on Man, making man live in his presence forever, for better context, live in him.

The Hebrew word for presence is "Shekhinah," which means dwelling. So, that something is present means it is dwelling, staying, inhabiting there. Now, it is important to note that you stay with someone doesn't automatically give you access to that person. Let's look at domestic staff [security guards, chefs, etc] that live with people, and this doesn't automatically give them access to their bosses/house owners. Access is gotten through a relationship. So these domestic staffs can even live in the quarters, not the main house. Here, we see that there are layers to ACCESS.

Thus, what has been happening to the believer is gross ignorance. We act like a girl child who hasn't been told she has a womb inside her that has provision to house a child to full term. Still, if she hasn't experienced childbirth, she may never really understand it. It's funny because, again, there are some documents that you need to sign. Some require a stamp or seal and signature, and others require a thumbprint. God's greatest signature on the earth is man because of his breath. He is FOREVER committed to us.

"What can separate us from the love of Christ?" Absolutely NOTHING, but the average believer is ignorant first of the fact that he is already in the presence of God. Thus, he cannot carry that consciousness of dominion as the highest signature of God & and, even greater, his partnership with him. So, the point of attention is largely not even the presence of God. God is already with you. The Holy Spirit is inside you and everything I've mentioned, but having access to the layers of his presence is needed to establish us as gods, like he said & ambassadors representing him.

Psalm 100:4 Enter his gates with thanksgiving; go into his courts with praise. Give thanks to him and praise his name. Acts 13:2 While they were worshiping the Lord and fasting, the Holy Spirit said, "Set apart for me Barnabas and Saul for the work to which I have called them." So David tells us that this is the key to access to an audience beyond just the atmosphere of his presence, and John records that while they were worshiping, The HOLY SPIRIT SPOKE. The proof that someone has a great relationship with you is comfortable sharing by speaking.

Our worship is a sacrifice of submission to him. Acknowledging him as ABBA. Hebrews 13:15 Through Him, therefore, let us always offer up to God a sacrifice of praise, which is the fruit of lips that thankfully acknowledge and confess and glorify His name. Our sacrifice of submission communicates self-insufficiency and our need for him, giving us access to dimensions of his presence that translate us to gods and sons of the most high to dominate just as he intended.

Thus, Dear Christian, this is my charge to you: You're already in his presence, but to walk in the consciousness of it, you have to put in more to be intentional about the father's heart through the sacrifice of a submitted self.

Write your own letter to God:

2ND LETTER
Consistency of God's Character

Dear Christian,

I've realized that as we examine different facets of life, we do not see the hand of God manifest. We just let them slide, eventually making us downplay a holistic approach to our Christian experience.

I'll start with your business. What did God say?

Psalm 1:3: "He shall be like a tree planted by the rivers of water, That brings forth its fruit in its season, Whose leaf also shall not wither; And whatever he does shall prosper." You know that God planted you in that business and gave you the idea, so what's happening? Why isn't it flourishing as it should? What questions aren't you asking?

Sick?

Matthew 8:17b: "He took our sicknesses and removed our diseases." If he took it, why do you have it? Why are you letting the devil camouflage a lie to you about your health status?

Faced with Challenges?

Isaiah 43:2, "When you pass through the waters, I will be with you; and when you pass through the rivers, they will not sweep over you. When you walk through the fire, you will not be burned; the flames will not set you ablaze." God is with you in the good times and even in the bad. He is not a fair-weather God. What you see as a challenge, he sees as a pruning process, the process of a miner, a sharpening effect on your character to make you come out as fine and purified gold. Thus, what perspective do you have of challenges and beyond God working through them? Are they normal and part of the process, or are they demonic? Again, is it consistent with God's character?

Are you not feeling loved enough?
Jer 31:3, "The LORD appeared to me (Lois) from ages past, saying, "I have loved you with an everlasting love; Therefore with lovingkindness, I have drawn you and continued My faithfulness to you." This line is rich from a book of love letters, the Bible—God's love poems to us. We are in the love of the Father, and to feel loved enough, sometimes we need to remind ourselves how much he loves us and walk in the consciousness of that.

Are you feeling forgotten and dejected?
Isaiah 49:16, "Indeed, I have inscribed [a picture of] you on the palms of My hands; Your city walls are continually before Me. Psalm 27:10: Even if my father and mother abandon me, the LORD will hold me close.

Are you struggling to complete/finish a phase or project?
Isaiah 66:9 "Shall I bring to the moment of birth and not give delivery?" says the LORD. "Or shall I who gives delivery shut the womb?" says your God." War with this scripture.

Ancestral curses/Threats?

Numbers 23:23: "For there is no sorcery against Jacob, Nor any divination against Israel. It now must be said of Jacob and Israel, 'Oh, what God has done!' Isaiah 49:25b I will contend with those who contend with you, and your children I will save.

Death?

Romans 8:38 For I am convinced that neither death nor life, neither angels nor demons, k neither the present nor the future, nor any powers, 39 neither height nor depth nor anything else in all creation, will be able to separate us from the love of God that is in Christ..."

The list can go on, but the goal is to look at what you're facing and ask, "IS THIS CONSISTENT WITH GOD'S CHARACTER?" Was this how he treated the patriarchs of old? Does this translate to the love he says he has for me?

Dear Christian, why aren't you asking those questions? 'I have said ye are gods, but my people will perish for lack of knowledge.' do those words sound familiar? Why are you keeping shut!!! OPEN YOUR MOUTH AND LET HIM FILL IT UP

You can trust consistency in the character of God, SPEAK THE WORD OVER THAT SITUATION, and TAKE HIS WORDS BACK TO HIM! ASK, AND YOU SHALL BE GIVEN! HE HAS ALREADY OPENED HIS HANDS AND SATISFIED OUR DESIRES!!!!

Dear Christian, be INTENTIONAL. SPEAK!!! ROAR!!! WAR!!!

Write your own letter to God:

3ʳᴰ LETTER
Faith

Dear Christian,

I was in a very difficult situation the first time: helpless, clueless, no idea. My room light turned off. I picked up my Bible and went to read Abraham's story. At least somebody can relate to me. Abraham was on his own; God called him.

He did not beg God, and he did not ask to be blessed. God promised him he would bless and give him a son, even make him a father of many nations. Okay, the son you eventually promised, you sent him at my very old age. It didn't end there, and you now said I should kill him. Is this playing?

I stopped there to understand how Abraham must have felt, and I cried my eyes out. The betrayal, the years lost, the trust, giving birth to a son out of the promise [Esau] just because it felt like the promise was taking too long. It's like, I trusted you all these years, and the son you promised over 20 years into walking with you, I should now kill him?

MAKE IT MAKE SENSE GOD! MAKE IT MAKE SENSE! But, wanting to kill Isaac, Abraham told his servant, "He said to his servants, "Stay here with the donkey while I and the boy go over there. We will worship, and then we will come back to you." Even in this speech, there was faith!

You're going to kill Isaac; how are you returning to him? Why are you calling your act of faith WORSHIP? The doggedness! The strong belief that God CAN, even in the face of despair, lacks clarity as to what he's doing, that he is doing something; thus, we remain at peace & trust.

As believers, the Bible is complete and can help us with ANY challenge. Our examples have already been set, and we have confidence that because God did it thousands of years ago, he only needs to replicate it.

"Follow them who through FAITH have obtained the promise." All the promises in the word hinged on FAITH to receive, but somehow, we can escape this dimension of the gospel. Sigh!

Dear Christian, Faith is NOT playing it safe! Faith is NOT logical! Faith is NOT having a backup plan! Faith is God taking us through a journey of trust in him. You can only run for so long. A time will come in your life when it is EITHER GOD or GOD!

Faith is a school that, as believers, we NEVER graduate from. When God called Abraham, He said to him come out of your father's house to the land. I will show you, and I will bless you. What land? But did Abraham ask that question? No.

So we are called to walk by FAITH and not by sight because we understand that even by faith, the creator formed the world with the words of his mouth. If God himself walks by faith, then who are we to think we can live up to the fullness of his purposes for us without FAITH?

Kingdom things are not chicken and chips/French fries. With the world, you work, invest, put in time and effort, and HOPE that it pays off gradually. It is only folly to think we would be laid back in Christ simply because Jesus can. He's not a magician!

Faith is a process, A journey! One that requires determination and consistency. God has said it! He is not uncertain, and HE WILL DO IT. So you travail with the word in PRAYER!

Relentless! No matter how long ELOHIM takes, he either does it or does it!

God's word has already met us halfway. He has already sent his word. We must travail to the point where we are changed to gods and sons of the most high, where our prayers match our stature in the spirit to authenticate our command.

Are you depending ENTIRELY on the word or ENTIRELY on God at the crux of whatever you want to pull through? Because it can be God with men doesn't mean it can be God & men. There's no in-between. You can't be lukewarm. Pick a struggle! But know FAITH will catch up with you. FAITH IS NOW, TARRY!!!

Write your own letter to God:

4ᵀᴴ LETTER
Christians as Salt

Dear Christian,

I was walking home one day when Lot's story came to my spirit & I was wondering, «But why pillar of salt?». I let it go. Today, I was praying, and it came again. So, I decided to read the story again.

Genesis 19

«Get them out of this place—your sons-in-law, sons, daughters, or anyone else. 13. For we are about to destroy this city completely. The outcry against this place is so great it has reached the LORD, who has sent us to destroy it.»

14. So Lot rushed out to tell his daughters› fiancés, «Quick, get out of the city! The LORD is about to destroy it.» But the young men thought he was only joking. C. Back story: Location, environment, and atmosphere are extremely important.

Genesis 13: 12-13

12. So Abram settled in the land of Canaan, and Lot moved his tents to a place near Sodom and settled among the cities of the plain. 13. But the people of this area were extremely wicked and constantly sinned against the LORD.

If the Bible recorded it, it was obvious Sodom was not good. Why did Lot still pitch his tent close to it? Apostle Joshua Selman will say infectious diseases don›t ask for your permission before they get to you. Jonah and the men on the ship are another excellent example where Jonah just had to be on the ship for all the misfortune against him to get to the other passengers.

Dear Christian, check your environment, location, and atmosphere. Who is toxic around you? Who drains your energy? Whose friend to your friend gives bad vibes? What location are you being invited to, and what place is it close to? Like your emotional energy, PROTECT YOUR SPIRITUAL ENERGY!

These things are not easy; there is no manual, and we have to ask the Holy Spirit for guidance, but let›s not give ourselves excuses when, like Lot, some things are obvious enough. This was later his undoing. A man who followed God raised his children close to evil.

The daughters eventually married men from Sodom, men that didn›t know God, and so we see as he gives them warning from the angel, they laugh at him, they don›t take him seriously, and are eventually left behind. As if this was not enough,

After leaving Sodom, his children got him drunk and slept with him. The ways of Sodom were already their lifestyle. They gave birth to Moab and Ben-Ammi, ancestors of the nations «Moabites and Ammonites,» we all know how these people troubled Israel.

Lot went from a man who knew God to his generation having nothing to write home about. All because he underestimated a threat to his walk with God. Like the

Apostle Paul would say, «Flee fornication.» Any potential threat to your Christian journey, Dear Christian, FLEE!!!

On our own, we can›t. On God›s own alone, he can›t because it›s a partnership, and some of us have coconut heads. So, the prayer remains the same, «to daily submit to him in fellowship, chase after his heart, and do his bidding.» This is the only escape route.

Finally, dear Christian, Reread some scriptures When you've laboured in the spirit. The degree of light and personal revelation you have is equivalent to the degree of capacity you have built. GROW, CONTEND FOR GROWTH, and KEEP GROWING.

Write your own letter to God:

5TH LETTER
The Holy Spirit and Prayer

Dear Christian,

I was at the "Koinonia Global" physical service in Abuja. I saw this man praying with his might; It wasn't his words for me, it was his countenance. And then I started thinking, "How did the disciples pray so much that there was visible fire on their heads"?

I decided to study further, and with the help of the Holy Spirit, I found some things. Acts 1: We see that Jesus resurrected and left them with the charge to wait for the comforter. Acts 2: the comforter comes like a mighty rushing wind.

You may not know that Pentecost day was 50 days after Easter, and in Acts 1, the Bible said, "The believers were constantly praying." There was a charge to wait for the comforter, but the attitude in their waiting was beyond waiting for him.

Praying and building capacity in the spirit, creating an altar to host his presence with their consistency in prayers. These people walked and worked with Jesus so the Holy Spirit could have come immediately. Why did he wait? Why did the disciples continue praying?

The funny thing is they didn't know when he would come, and they only knew Jesus said he would come. Sometimes, when it seems God is taking the time to answer your prayers, he needs to translate you to a dimension that befits the answer. Spiritually first and then physically.

Luke 9:29-30 As he was praying, the appearance of his face changed, and his clothes became as bright as a flash of lightning. Two men, Moses and Elijah, appeared in glorious splendour, talking with Jesus. The translation that comes with certain heights in prayer.

Two months of consistent prayer!!! And the Holy Spirit said yes, they've replicated my atmosphere; I can now come and do what I want to do in the dimension I want. Then he came Loud!!! He came with power that brought speed and visibility to the body of Christ;

So much so that 3,000 people were added to the church, you, small worship, you'll cry, wail, "Jesus, I want more of you. All your emotions will come out as if, if Jesus doesn't come, you can die." You step out of the church, and the next thing you're back at that secret sin or that habit...

You've prayed for one week, STAY. Two weeks, and you're tired already. STAY Three weeks, and it's like God, is it only me? STAY Three months, and it's like God, when will you show up? STAY One year, and you're saying, what's the point, STAY.

He's building your evidence, and when he shows up, he's coming with power and speed that'll transform your life, making you an effective witness because no other testimony bears witness like a breathing one.

Dear Christian

Write your own letter to God:

6ᵀᴴ LETTER
Psalm 23

Dear Christian,

Let›s talk about Psalm 23 and how powerful this Psalm is.
1. The Lord is my shepherd; I have everything I need.
2: He maketh me to lie down in green pastures: he leadeth me beside the still waters. When you lie down, you rest; you›re at peace. Pastures are rich enough that animals graze in them. Thus, Christ makes you rest in the richness of the earth and leads you through peaceful waters

Summarily, he makes you at rest with the elements of this old earth. He makes you in sync with it as he leads you. The earth has no right to not yield its increase to you.

3: He restoreth my soul: he leadeth me in the paths of righteousness for his name's sake.

Your soul consists of your mind, will, and intellect. Everything that makes for mental capacity and comprehension PHYSICALLY. Thus, He restores, continuously refreshes your being, and leads you on the right path for his sake because you represent him.

4: Yea, though I walk through the valley of the shadow of death, I will fear no evil: for thou art with me; thy rod and thy staff comfort me. His staff protects us from ourselves when we stray from him. His rod protects us from the enemies.

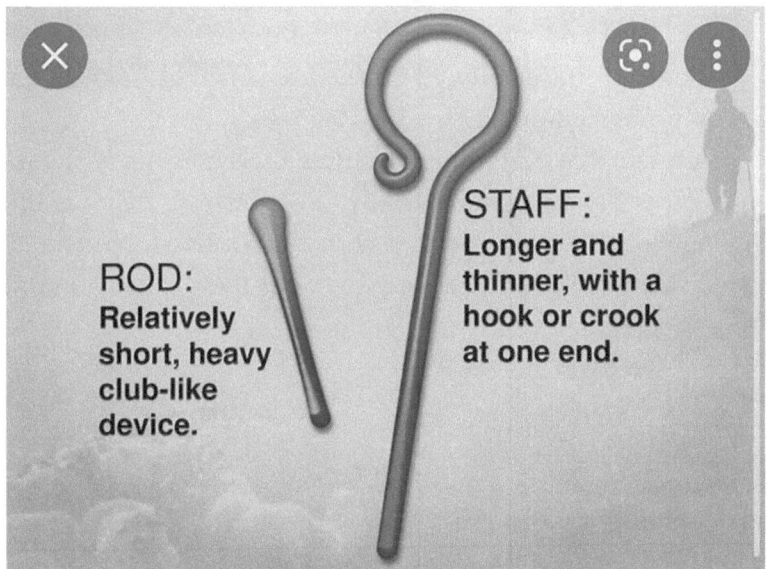

Like we see our shadow, when it looks like the earth mirrors death, challenges, and storms, we fear nothing because he is with us. In the fire, he will not let us burn; in the water, he won›t let us drown because he is the floater that we bank on, the fourth man that makes the fire cold.

5: Thou preparest a table before me in the presence of mine enemies: thou anoints my head with oil; my cup runneth over. The audacity for me. He prepares a meal of life and lays it out for me. A meal of his numerous dimensions: Grace, favour, wisdom, glory, peace, joy, speed, etc. He doesn›t stop there and sits with me amidst the enemies watching. They cannot taste it; they can›t stop me from eating it. Then he puts a seal on me with the oil he anoints me with that exalts my head like a unicorn's horn, and my life starts looking like an outpouring of his blessings.

6: Surely, goodness and mercy shall follow me all the days of my life: and I will dwell in the house of the LORD forever. Certainly, it is a MUST that I will wake up to expressions of his goodness and mercy every day of my life.

These promises hinged on the premise that I would stay in his presence forever.

A psalm that underlines promises in partnership with God and Us as believers individually. The promise of Jesus in a lifelong leadership partnership with our positive submission as we make him Lord and master over our lives. What a Psalm!

Write your own letter to God:

7TH LETTER

The Believer's cure for fear.

Dear Christian,

I came across Pastor Tony Rapu›s Shekere concert on YouTube and decided to listen.

Let›s talk about the cure for fear in the life of a believer.

While worshiping and praying with it, the popular song came up in the worship, «No longer a slave to fear.» One of the prayers I said sporadically was, «No longer scared of the unknown, no what-ifs.» Then I paused. Listening to the song like I›ve never heard it. This was light.

Towards the end of the original song, «I'm no longer a slave to fear, I am a child of God (full of faith)," made the scriptures come ", And this is the victory that overcometh the world, even our faith" and another scripture "…for the perfect love has no fear and whoever fears have not been made perfect in love."

In clear terms, the opposite of fear is faith, and whoever fears has not understood the love of God enough to walk in it to dispel fear. Then I thought of couples that cuddle, especially when the man is holding the lady close, the sense of protection, safety & love communicated.

Psalm 91:4 is how God cuddles us: "He will cover you with his feathers. He will shelter you with his wings. His faithful promises are your armour and protection."

2 Kings 6:16-17 "Don't be afraid," the prophet answered. "Those who are with us are more than those who are with them."

17. Elisha prayed, "Open his eyes, Lord, so that he may see." Then the Lord opened the servant's eyes, and he looked and saw the hills full of horses and chariots of fire all around Elisha. ...

Dear Christian, Why are you afraid? What are you afraid of?

Fear of the unknown? He knows tomorrow.

What ifs? He said all things will work together for your good.

For he that cometh to him MUST BELIEVE THAT HE IS AND HE IS A REWARDER OF THEM WHO DILIGENTLY SEEK HIM.

Brings us to valid questions. "Are your eyes opened? Are you looking but not seeing? What lenses are you using to view the love of God for you?"

Write your own letter to God:

8ᵀᴴ LETTER
Waiting and Dominion

Dear Christian,

If you've been waiting on God for something, you need to know this.

So, The Holy Spirit was telling me the above is the ideal setting. However, God has met us already; "he has rested from his works," and now, he is waiting for us to meet him.

Hebrews 4:3 Now we who have believed enter that rest, just as God has said, "So I declared on oath in my anger, 'They shall never enter my rest.'" And yet his works have been finished since the creation of the world.

This is where WAITING and DOMINION come in because you can't be translated to the image of God without waiting in his presence. He that "dwells," "stays," and WAITS continuously in the secret place is translated to a god.

The Holy Spirit said dominion can be achieved when our waiting brings translation, and then this translation elevates us to the position God has truly ordained for us. The position in Hebrews 2:6-8 "…What is mankind that you are mindful of them, a son of man that you care for him?

7. You made them a little a lower than the angels; you crowned them with glory and honour 8. and put everything under their feet." In putting everything under them, God left nothing that is not subject to them…"

When we're translated to this position by our consistent waiting, we meet God. He talks to us as people he kept in charge of the earth. At this point, we don't even need to ask him for anything. Matthew 6:33 becomes automatic.

"But seek first his kingdom and righteousness, and all these things will be given to you as well." So, to some people waiting on God, tired, frustrated, needing something urgent from him, it's okay because you're human. Today, I've come to bring light.

Change your perspective of what you see waiting to be. The same applies to people tired of pastors prophesying, who don't see the manifestation of the prophesy. Yes, at times, divine intervention can take place by the mercy of God.

However, like Paul said in Hebrews 5:13-14

13. Anyone who lives on milk, still an infant, is not acquainted with the teaching about righteousness.

14. But solid food is for the mature, who have trained themselves to distinguish good from evil by constant use.

Not every time prophecy or divine intervention will work because God will not pamper you.

So, Dear Christian who wants to keep taking milk, recognize that if you don't translate to solid food, God will use uncomfortable situations to move you.

If you recognize what God is doing and start complying with him, amazing. If you don't, you'll continue being frustrated. It's not truly about what you want with God because he can give it to you. He has already given it to you. However, he needs to use your need to get you to the position where you can have access to your desires and more. A place beyond just your need but giving you dominion to never need, to have earth answer to you as an AMBASSADOR for Christ.

Dear Christian, God has already met us. He's waiting for us to meet him. SELAH

Write your own letter to God:

9TH LETTER

The Trinity and love

Dear Christian

I was worshiping when the Holy Spirit started speaking to my heart.

Singles, Almost Married, Married, everybody, get in here.

With the help of the Holy Spirit, I created this diagram, which we'll be using for context. It'll help to read side by side.

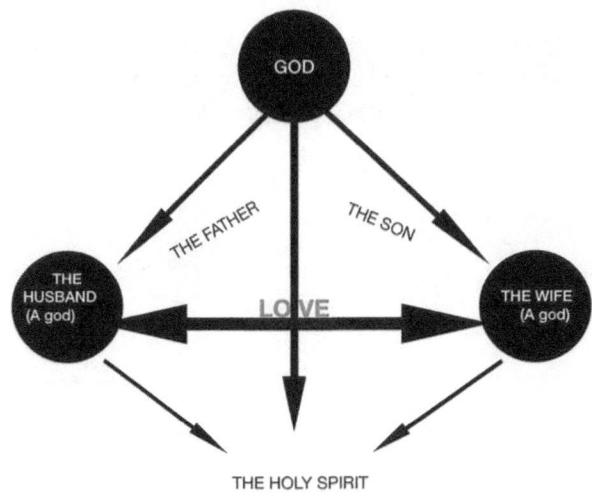

LOIS TARIKABOR'S TRINITY AND LOVE

John 1:1 In the beginning was the Word, and the Word was with God, and the Word was God. Gen 2:21 So the LORD God caused the man to fall into a deep sleep. While the man slept, the LORD God took out one of the man's ribs and closed up the opening.

Gen2: 22 Then the LORD God made a woman from the rib, and he brought her to the man. 23"At last!" the man exclaimed. "This one is bone from my bone and flesh from my flesh! She will be called 'woman' because she was taken from 'man.'"

Adam was not awake when God was taking out the rib, so he didn't know what it looked like or that Eve was formed out of his rib. In prophesy, when Adam saw EVE, he exclaimed by the spirit, this is the bone from my bone and the flesh from my flesh.

I believe Adam in the flesh knew Eve had his features, but let's talk about the formation. Looking at the rib diagram, it's all made up of bones. How did God use bones to make flesh and bones again, then make the body different from man?

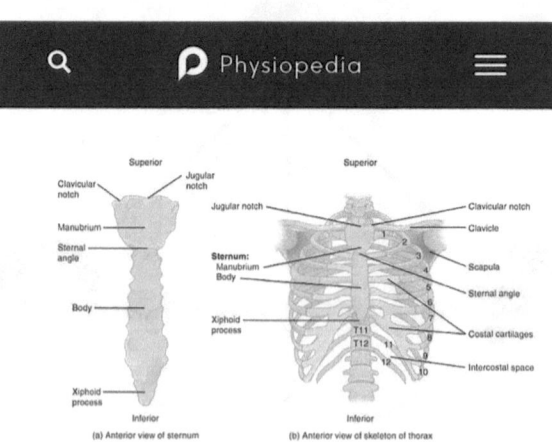

The ribs are the bony framework of the thoracic cavity.

This is the concept of the Trinity. God the Father, God the Son, and God the Holy Spirit. All of God's heads are separate but share one will and one purpose, and together, they are called God.

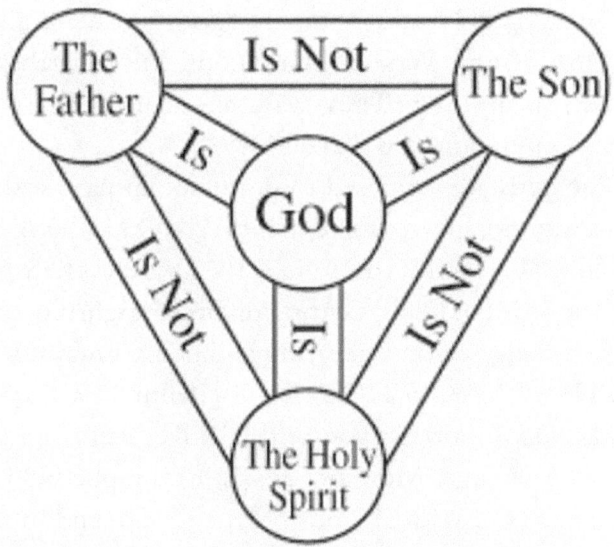

Trinity in the New Testament
catholic-resources.org

So, God did the same thing for Adam. First, he creates Adam from dust and puts his breath in him. Then he makes him sleep, takes something out of him, and puts it in the woman. Putting an attribute of himself to both the man and woman.

The end goal is to highlight love! When John said God is Love, he meant God the Father is love. God the Son is love. God, the Holy Spirit, is love. 1st Corinthians 13:13 And now these three remain faith, hope, and love. But the greatest of these is love.

Love is the whole essence of life, the key. So when a man loves a woman and vice versa, in and through Christ, they use love to unlock the power of the Trinity in them. They dominate! and the devil knows this. That's why he fights for unity in marriage.

Psalm 82:6: "I said, 'You are "gods"; you are all sons of the Most High.' Verse 5: The 'gods' know nothing; they understand nothing. They walk about in darkness; all the earth's foundations are shaken.

The gods are supposed to dominate in partnership with the Trinity as a greater force. KNOW NOTHING! They are ignorant, WALKING ABOUT IN DARKNESS (no light from the word of God), Getting divorced, fighting, marrying for the wrong reasons, cheating and being unfaithful,

"THEY KNOW NOTHING" Psalm 82:7, But you will die like mere mortals; you will fall like every other ruler." Beyond Marriage, Matthew 22:37, Jesus replied: "'Love the Lord your God with all your heart and soul and mind.'

38. This is the first and greatest commandment. 39. The second is like it: 'Love your neighbour as yourself.' The understanding of the love you have for God is what you'll interpret in your life and, in extension, give to your neighbor.

This is the greatest commandment because if people loved their neighbours like themselves, they wouldn't do things that hurt other people, knowing fully well if the tables were turned, they would be hurt, too.

So, in 1 Corinthians 13:13, these three remain faith, hope, and love. But the greatest of these is love. Like John, the Beloved said: 1 John 4:16… God is love. Whoever lives in love lives in God, and God in them.

Psalm 23:1 - The Lord is my shepherd, I have all I need. If God is enough and he is love, Love is enough! The entirety of a concept is not limited to your scope or understanding of it.

There is no true love! There is no genuine love! Stop using the qualities of love to define it. Love is true genuine, and love is the KEY TO LIFE.

Dear singles, soon to be married, married, EVERYBODY! It is my prayer that you trust God for understanding. LOVE IS ENOUGH, but it is dependent on your understanding of it. Thus the real question you should think about "What do you know about love?"

Write your own letter to God:

10TH LETTER
A positive Life

Dear Christian,

Mark 12:30-31
30. And you must love the Lord your God with all your heart, all your soul, all your mind, and all your strength.'
31. The second is equally important: 'Love your neighbour as yourself. No other commandment is greater than these."

The hierarchy will always be understanding God's love for man and channeling that to loving yourself. When this is done, loving your neighbour becomes seamless.

Truly, if understood, this is the summation of a positive life across all people because the cycle of understanding is NOT broken. Someone did something to me, and I was slightly upset and thinking over it.

I got home and headed for my therapy session (a hot shower and worship or praise playing for 20-30 minutes)

P.S. Try this and thank me later for showing you how to do/stress, deposit worship and praise in your spirit, get ideas, hear God, etc.) Back to the gist...

I was in the shower when I thought, "If he loved me like he loved himself and not lesser if this person was kind to me..." After all, love is kind!

Getting into this year, I told God I didn't want any emotional stress. I want rest and peace of mind, and anything that wants to contradict that, and he should take it away. On my path, anything I see as a threat to it, things that'll make me worked up, I take it out.

So, while In the shower, I decided to be more INTENTIONAL about being kind to people. I thought of people I've given to and helped that won't be paying me back and how I'm about to do it again. Then I said, well, you might as well start a tradition.

As with my prayer wall, I ordered a To do board from Amazon. Monthly Headings will be Acts of Kindness, Giving, and Goals. It's the little things that make you feel wholesome, heal your heart subconsciously, and make you glow from within. I'm excited

I imagine myself standing back with a full board, grinning ear to ear, and saying, "Thank you, Jesus; we blessed people, warmed people's hearts, and made people smile. We inspired little hope and maybe sowed a seed:" It'll always be the little things.

Highlighted Notes: Understanding God's love for man and channeling that understanding to loving yourself. When this is done, loving your neighbor becomes seamless.

Write your own letter to God:

11ᵀᴴ LETTER
Growth in Christ

Dear Christian,

More often than not, when we are faced with a challenge as Christians, it feels foreign because we sometimes think that because we're Christians and Christ rules the world, all our troubles are to disappear automatically, and we will have a smooth scale through life. However, see it as this. Your Christian status does not make money appear in your account; you've got to work. You've got to get up, shower, commute, and learn, and if you must grow to higher positions in your place of work, you've got to put in the effort. Christianity is not that different because you must still partner with Christ. As a factor, you are important in the equation, and your willingness to work with God along your journey counts for a better life.

Every challenge or tough time allows you to grow in spirit and build capacity. This is not to say God cannot immediately give us what we ask, but there is often spiritual growth, physical growth, God's timing, and purpose because the Bible says man's heart is wicked; we know this world is wicked. Thus, if we are to withstand this wickedness and even be a light in the darkness for others to follow, which will, in turn, point them to Christ, God has to build and train us.

The Bible says in Hebrews 5:13-14 "Anyone who lives on milk, being still an infant, is not acquainted with the teaching about righteousness. 14. But solid food is for the mature, who have trained themselves to distinguish good from evil by constant use."

So, as baby Christians, we start learning, listening to messages, trying to abide, letting go of our old nature, looking more to Jesus, and being transformed into his image and likeness. Slowly and gradually, we find that we're more mature emotionally; as we study the word, we see a mental transformation and a working in us. Our character is furnished unto good works, our prayer life thorough, our obedience unhindered. We get to where God can trust us with things, people, and his program. The testimony of us, exported to the nations for Jesus to be seen and glorified.

All of these happen with time, challenges that God will help us overcome even as he teaches us valuable lessons through them. This is how we are changed and grow in Christ. Not to our detriment but for profiting that we may become worthy Christian ambassadors.

Write your own letter to God:

12TH LETTER
Youthing for Christ

Dear Christian,

LOOK AROUND!
More-so,
DEAR WOKE YOUTH,

Let me draw your attention in case you haven't noticed.

The devil thought he was destroying us with "wokeness" to turn our backs on kingdom practices and lifestyle.

True, God allowed him to have his fill for some time.

Then, God brought in his reverse psychology. So the demand from the woke youth to truly understand the scriptures and the curiosity to experience the workability of scriptural truths have been met with dynamic revelations from the spirit, Berean Christians;

Young Christians who want to experience power and touch spiritual realities. They do not blindly follow religion, go to church every day, and watch their destinies suffer. Christians sense and know that there is more and want to experience more.

Now more than ever, in the coming years, it is going to be huge!

Romans 8:18-19**18**

I consider that our present sufferings are not worth comparing with the glory that will be revealed in us. **19** For the creation waits eagerly for the children of God to be revealed.

Godly lifestyle, Christian doctrines, and practices are being understood through the lens of the spirit. Christians are partnering with God to fulfill their purpose in the industry he has called them, and oh, CHRIST IS WINNING!

We're moving beyond "What church do you attend?" to let us pray for the kingdom, how can we strengthen the body, what role do I need to play, and how can I be a blessing? Look around; if you're not on this side, start re-tracing your steps because, slowly but surely, we will dominate!

Matthew 6:33 says

But seek first his kingdom and righteousness, and all these things will also be given to you.

So ask yourself,

What am I doing for God?

How have I blessed humanity as a result of my Christianity?

How have I helped to spread the love of Christ abroad?

What gap am I filling?

Where does God need for me?

How can I participate in the kingdom agenda of heaven on earth?

Write your own letter to God:

13TH LETTER

The fruits of the Spirit

Dear Christian,

Galatians 5:22-23

But the fruit of the Spirit is love, joy, peace, forbearance, kindness, goodness, faithfulness,

23. gentleness and self-control. Against such things, there is no law.

Sometime in July 2021, I was searching for more, and I remember reading my Bible and saying I was going for a three-day night prayer journey. By the third day, I heard 40 days. Can I be "unheard," please, because of what happened? However, I obeyed.

This meant that I had to set my alarm multiple times and keep my light on (the hardest sacrifice for me), but these were necessary checks, so I was not so comfortable sleeping. I would spend about thirty minutes praying, speaking in tongues, and worshipping.

Then, for the last 30 minutes, just praise as instructed. Before the 40th day was over, I heard clearly in my spirit, you'll never be sad. I already decided not to, but I didn't know the extent.

Praise has been my lifestyle for some time. I got back from work excited and wanting to praise God for everything he has done for me. Then he showed me what he meant in July. I hardly ever worry. Yes, sometimes I get anxious. I try to know the next plan, and even when I'm that way, my spirit brings a song, and the next thing, I'm singing, I'm dancing In the open, my hands are in the air, I'm turning around at work and even on streets. If there were hidden cameras that take videos anytime I do this, it's crazy. I don't know how to hide my joy; I don't want to.

It's funny how nothing new may have happened, but yet I'm rejoicing just like that. Indeed, obedience to a sacrifice plugged me into the Lord's joy, giving me strength to thrive throughout this year. And so the Holy Spirit was trying to tell me today...

"You sowed the seed, Lois." For fruits to be seen, the seed must be sown. Likewise, the fruits of the spirit. Love; try expressing it through giving, Joy, praise, Peace, and faith. I think these main three are the pillars that the others stand on and the Help of the Holy Spirit. When we bear these fruits, our character is moulded to the image of Christ because as we behold him, we become. Attaining godliness, to the end that life becomes doable in Christ & abundant life even more attainable.

May our spirits sing songs, may they take us to realms, may they explain bliss to us unimaginably, and may people glorify Jesus because of us.

Write your own letter to God:

14TH LETTER

Food from The Spirit

Dear Christian,

1ˢᵗ Kings 19

Elijah ran away for his dear life due to Jezeebel's threat. Jezebel must have been something because Elijah just made raintofall after 3 years plus. With so much power, he was so scared of Jezebel's threat that he had to run away for his life.

He's thinking of spending a day in the wilderness when God hears his frustration: "I have had enough, Lord, take my life; I am no better than my ancestors." God sends an angel to give him food and prepare him for a journey.

Elijah didn't even know it was a journey he was embarking on until the angel came the second time. "Then the angel of the LORD came again, touched him, and said, "Get up and eat some more, or the journey ahead will be too much for you."

Now, I think the angel gave Elijah the food, which was "just" bread and water in two meals that sustained him for 40 days. "So he got up and ate and drank, and the food gave him enough strength to travel forty days and forty nights to Mount Sinai."

As simple as a meal, bread, and water, Elijah was sustained for 40 days and nights. So God has told you or is trying to tell you to "eat" for the journey is far (challenging, long), and he's giving you the bread from the spirit by quickening you to pray, fast, speak in tongues, praise, etc.

But you're probably rejecting this meal that looks simple but can sustain you. Like Elijah, he's trying to separate you from the fear and doubts that have made things not work out, and after he does that and has equipped you, he'll tell you.

"Go back the same way you came and travel to the wilderness of Damascus." He'll tell you, let's face that challenge with the new arsenals you've gotten. But you must eat first; whatever the extent of your journey, it's life, so by default, it's already far.

Write your own letter to God:

15TH LETTER
Your Purpose is your worship.

Dear Christian

I was lying on the floor outside my friend's house. Enjoying the breeze & just catching up. All of a sudden, my eyes were fixed on the clouds. A couple of days back, I was reading the creation story with the background music "So Will I," which I think is the most poetic piece of worship.

I have been trying so hard to see something different in this story. Today, it came! Clouds, stars, and nature worship by staying in their purpose, by doing what they are meant to do given to them by God. "Let us worship God in spirit and truth."

The truth is his word; the spirit is his spirit that backs up his word and brings it into physical manifestation, giving it life. So beyond singing songs, yes, worship is supposed to be a lifestyle, but YOUR LIFESTYLE SHOULD WORSHIP. (2 different things)

When our life worships God, when we stay in God's purpose for us, he inhabits us as he inhabits the praises of his people and colours our lives.

I was looking at the clouds, and suddenly, I told my friend, "How do people say God Doesn't exist? How can this be explained? And then light cams. Worship is an honour, worship is respect, worship is reverence, and worship is obedience.

When your lifestyle worships and you walk in God's purpose for you, he inhabits you. Look at the heaven, the bliss, because the angels and 24 elders always worship. That's how your life becomes. Help us, Lord Jesus.

Write your own letter to God:

16ᵀᴴ LETTER
Spiritual Bank

Dear Christian,

What is in your spiritual bank?
A deep thread from the wisdom of the Holy Spirit.

After my koinonia meeting, I got into a cab to go home, and this lady got in. Almost immediately, she says, "I'm happy I got in with you 'cause I don't have money to pay." I WAS IRRITATED! However, I had to submit a favour.

I smiled and told her, "So why did you get in if you don't have money to pay?" She says, "Is this your first time being to Koinonia? I'm like no. I recalled when the apostle said, "talk to men with respect but audacity that they'll favour you." I was irritated, but I paid for her!

I paid because I had the understanding. Fast forward to later that week; I'm in a cab getting home from work. The man beside me gives me a stare. He's about to alight the car and tells the driver he's paying for everybody. Steps down and continues looking at me.

This simple act made me realize that life CAN be cycles of favour or anything depending on your mindset. When the Bible said, "Give, and it will be given unto you," it wasn't only money being talked about. Continuous giving unlocks a portal of what is given.

> Ecc 11:1-2 Cast your bread upon the waters,
> for you will find it after many days.
> 2Give a portion to seven, or even to eight,
> for you know not what disaster may happen on earth.

So because giving is a spiritual principle, you give in the physical, and the spiritual gets an ALERT of your act. In understanding, you call forth those things that are not as though they were (placing a demand on your spiritual bank)

And the spirit takes from your reserve and summons the elements of nature that answer to it. Be its favour, be it an honour. As long as there is a reserve in the spirit, the spirit brings it out and ensures a physical manifestation. Always pray so that in the days your strength is small, the prayers you've sent ahead will speak for you. Love, show mercy, be kind, and let the spirit's fruit show in you. All of these and more are investments. So, in summary, make spiritual investments.

Write your own letter to God:

17TH LETTER
Emotions in Worship

Dear Christian,

I was engaging in a particular spiritual activity and wasn't "feeling" the spirit. I wasn't hearing anything speaking inside me, no "goose bumps". I started saying to myself -God, are you sure I shouldn't even stop halfway like this. Hours later, I was at Koinonia, and the voice came.

Whether it be taking d communion or prayer/fasting or praising, it's not because of what you're doing that the principle works: "Our righteousness is after all filthy" 2corinth 5: 21 God made him who had no sin to be sin for us, so that in him we might become the righteousness of God.

The principle works because of 1. The honour you placed on it. 2. Intent (Rom 8:27a And he who searches our hearts knows the mind of the Spirit) ... So sometimes the devil tries to deceive you...

You say you're fasting, but you insulted this person in your heart. You're taking communion, but you told your friend to take drugs...bla bla bla The Holy Spirit knows your true motive and intentions and filters everything through the righteousness of Christ.

And No, seek his presence before goosebumps. The Holy Spirit is beyond the physiological showmanship of hormones reacting. God is a loving and faithful father. Slow to anger and continuously knocking on the doors of our hearts.

Write your own letter to God:

18ᵀᴴ LETTER

The Aroma of Worship

Dear Christian,

Have you heard 'Bow Down and Worship' by Benjamin Dube and Praise Explosion, preferably the life rendition? The first part of the chorus of the song states:
"Consuming fire, sweet perfume, his awesome presence feels this room..."
Once, there was a sacrifice in the Bible, and God called it "aroma."
Romans 12:1: "And so, dear brothers and sisters, I plead with you to give your bodies to God because of all he has done for you. Let them be a living and holy sacrifice—the kind he will find acceptable. This is truly the way to worship him".
This talks about our bodies as a sacrifice, which in turn is our worship, which sends an aroma to God, but here's another side…
Body Odour can result from physical activity, triggering the body to produce sweat, rubbing off on your pubic hairs, and you start to smell. Our sacrifice and aroma trigger the Holy Spirit IN US when we worship.

Like an aroma, his presence embodies and saturates us, and oh, the benefits of his presence that attract favour, blessing, glory, Grace, etc. In Psalm 91:1, the Bible records that He that dwelleth in the secret place shall abide under the shadow of God.

His presence becomes a covering. When people see us, they see him because a shadow can't be different from its owner. That our lifestyle be the sacrifice and our mortal bodies, the host for the altar. Thus, when we surrender the lifestyle of flesh to the lifestyle of the spirit, DAILY remaining in him, our sacrifice continues to burn in our altars. The fire never goes out.

The reason why Paul said in Romans 12:2 "Don't copy the behaviour and customs of this world, but let God transform you into a new person by changing the way you think. Then you will learn to know God's will for you, which is good and pleasing and perfect."

The more we behold him, the more we are changed & transformed to look like him. We worship first with our lifestyle and bodies, surrendering to his will and desires. This is the kind he finds acceptable. This is what precedes songs and Thanksgiving. The entirety, WHOLESOME WORSHIP.

Dear Lord, The grace to receive help to act accordingly. To not just hear but do.

If God ever drops a song in your spirit, please listen and worship him with it. He's kept a message in it for you; as you yield, he'll cause a working and perfection.

Write your own letter to God:

19TH LETTER

Christ in Us

Dear Christian

David Dam sang a song with the lyrics, "I am under the shadow of his wings, his influence is over me."

A lot of things, when seen in the flesh, look unachievable. It could be an addiction, sexual immorality, a bad habit, etc. When you're under the influence of alcohol, you're clueless about your actions—likewise, being under the influence of the Holy Spirit.

Gal 2:20

I have been crucified with Christ [that is, in Him, I have shared His crucifixion]; it is no longer I who live, but Christ lives in me. The life I now live in the body I live by faith [by adhering to, relying on, and completely trusting] in the Son of God, who loved me and gave Himself up for me.

Overcoming flesh with flesh takes us nowhere. If we're being honest, we go around our sins in the same cycle. The devil makes the cycles look different, whereas it's the same vehicle we're driving through them.

And yes, it takes discipline to submit to the authority of the Holy Spirit before the place of grace. So you already know it's going to take some sacrifice; it's going to cost you.

Then again, like Jesus, who paid the price on the cross for the greater glory,

Not all our losses are actual losses. Some are tests to see how much our eyes are fixed on the latter and how much we're willing to let go of our deepest desires in line with God's will.

Ultimately, Christ in Us is the hope of glory, and this is my charge to you from Paul in his address to the church in Corinth;

2 Corinth 4:16-18

16. Therefore, we do not lose heart. Though outwardly we are wasting away, yet inwardly, we are being renewed day by day. **17** For our light and momentary troubles are achieving for us an eternal glory that far outweighs them all. **18** we fix our eyes not on what is seen, but on what is unseen, since what is seen is temporary, but what is unseen is eternal.

Trust that Christ in you is greater, and hold on to that thought with every fiber of your being.

Write your own letter to God:

20ᵀᴴ LETTER
How love is Supposed to be

Dear Christian,

I was praying today, and out of nowhere, I said, "To love you just like you have loved me, to put you first just like you put me first."

Then I paused because what were these words!!!

Then the Holy Spirit said, "Isn't that how love is supposed to be? I have your best interest at heart; you have my best interest at heart."

And yes, we could never be God, be like or love him in the same measure. And yes, he alone can determine our hearts; if we love him as we say...

But today, I just felt that with this love affair with God, he's grossly cheated on a large scale. People cheat on their partners, and they get caught, heartbroken, hurt, disappointed, give an attitude, etc.

Do we give God time to process his feelings? Do we think he's even "allowed" to give an attitude? We cheat on him, come back, he takes us, next thing, okay, I want this, I want that... Aren't we supposed to take time out to bond with him again and please his heart?

Is this cheesy? Well yeah. Am I God's spokesman? No. Well, he created us in his image, and we do not have a high priest who cannot empathize with our weaknesses, but we have one who has been tempted in every way, just as we are—yet he did not sin.

Maybe sometimes he even says I have loved you with an everlasting love. I show you how I bless you for people to see, but when it's my turn ... I don't know, guys, I'm just going on some love discourse in my head. Romeo and Juliet... Jesus and the church... Romeo, Jesus & Juliet...Whatever you make of this in tandem with your love life with Jesus.

Write your own letter to God:

21ST LETTER

Humanity, even in Christ

Dear Christian

2 Corinthians 12:8
Three times, I pleaded with the Lord to take it away from me. 9 But he said to me, "My grace is sufficient for you, for my power is made perfect in weakness." Therefore, I will boast all the more gladly about my weaknesses so that Christ's power may rest on me.

Fast and pray all you want. Ultimately, the truth remains that "YOU'RE STILL HUMAN!" I was talking to a friend about an issue, and after that, I was thinking to myself and laughed out loud, then started talking to myself, "God, it has to be you."

You'll find yourself in situations where you'll say, "God, are you sure? Should I go ahead? Is it your will? You're not saying anything now oo. I don't like your silence. At the same time, I don't like how I feel…sigh."

But I'm glad I realized early that life will ALWAYS give you what you want in Christ. Continuously stay in him, be focused, and press in. Eventually, everything works out. Earth mirrors your energy. IN CHRIST, ANYTHING is possible. Abundant life is inclusive.

"What heights of love, what depths of peace, where fears are stilled, where striving to seize. My comforter, my all in all, here in the love of Christ, I stand!"

Write your own letter to God:

22ND LETTER
Focusing on the Intimate Love of Christ

Dear Christian,

Yes, binding and casting are good, but sometimes, you need to focus on the love of the father. Beyond his blessings and promises, there is a need to acknowledge to him expressly that you see his love in action.

Sometimes, you need your emotions strengthened to function, even to pray and get through the day. We ignore these things and see them as little, but they are the pillars that make us stand. In them, God sees our most sincere need of him, answers, and uplifts us.

And so now and then, prayers could be songs, hymns of love, acknowledgement, etc. As simple as things like singing, "Yes Jesus loves me, the bible tells me so…" insert some lines of acknowledgement. You said in Hosea 2:16, "No longer will I call you master but husband," "Not even angels can come between the love you have for me," "You have loved me with an everlasting love," and I know you think of me. I know you're smiling now, yes, cause you're looking at my name engraved in your palm, standing out as you think of your purpose for me.

And so even as I sleep, breathe upon me and give me rest. Wrap me in your outstretched arms and comfort me; hug me so tight that I wake up to a strong aroma of your glory all around me. Oh, the bliss! Yes, prayer is intimate, but do you pray in intimate prayers?

While you think about that, it'll be helpful to meditate on Romans 8: 35-38 **35.** Can anything ever separate us from Christ's love? Does it mean he no longer loves us if we have trouble or calamity, or are persecuted, or hungry, or destitute, or in danger, or threatened with death? **36** (As the Scriptures say, "For your sake we are killed every day; we are being slaughtered like sheep."o) **37** No, despite all these things, overwhelming victory is ours through Christ, who loved us.38And I am convinced that nothing can ever separate us from God's love. Neither death nor life, neither angels nor demons, p neither our fears for today nor our worries about tomorrow—not even the powers of hell can separate us from God's love. **39** No power in the sky above or in the earth below—indeed, nothing in all creation will ever be able to separate us from the love of God that is revealed in Christ Jesus our Lord.

God's love is enough for you to succeed in life, but you're simply not basking in it. He led the example and showed us what love looks like. He gave his only begotten son. He went ahead to tell us "perfect love, cast out fear" in 1 John 4:18 and several other verses;

"Cast your cares upon me," "I will never leave you nor forsake you," "I have loved you with an everlasting love," "You are the apple of mine eyes," "Who is the man that you are mindful of him?" ...

Love is the foundation of the new covenant upon which Christianity is hinged. It was still at the center of the old. Love Conquers All because God is Love. Too many assurances of God's love. Stop being insecure about his love. It's a perfect love with a perfect God. Walk in it.

Write your own letter to God:

23ʳᵈ LETTER
Spiritual Inferiority

Dear Christian,

I don't particularly appreciate talking about spiritual activities I engage in. Just pass the message across and be alright. I don't want people to know how much I'm spiritual.

Coupled with the idea that the Christian journey is personal (deceit). Yes, you grow at your own pace, but if you're not spreading the good news, how are you the world's light and salt of the earth?

Then again, I saw something recently on spiritual inferiority, and well, I think I should start plugging out of that. I fast once every week, depending on the phase and period I'm in. If there's a program, I go with their schedule and so on.

I fasted one day, and you're supposed to be connected in fasting. Studying the word, worship, tongues, etc. I didn't do anyone for most of it; I was working on this new project I started and was on my laptop for long hours. Time to break the fast...

I said, "God, what kind of fast did I do? Maybe I should just eat and fast tomorrow", but my spirit said I should continue my prayers. I was inclined to speak in tongues. I went to my worship and tongues playlist and started.

Into the prayer, the Holy Spirit was directing as usual. All of a sudden, I heard Mary. Hmmm, what about Mary? I'm reading Ezekiel (Tongues were still going on). Then I heard, "And the power of the most high shall overshadow you." Then Mary said, "Be it unto me according to your word."

The Holy Spirit started explaining (Tongues, we're still going on) The power of the most high being, the glory of God, overshadowed Mary, and the result was John 1:14: "The word became flesh..." We see the strange physical possibilities...

(A pregnant Virgin) manifested from the glory of God AND the submission of Mary to the will of the Father. The Holy Spirit is saying these strange possibilities can happen to us. Explicitly, it is written, "He that dwelleth in the secret place of the most high shall abide under the shadow of the Almighty."

In simple terms, staying in God's presence/his glory acts as a covering, and then you can place a demand. It doesn't necessarily have to be you placing a demand because in the secret place is where he reveals his will for you to you. Once you agree to work with him in carrying it out, those strange possibilities that seem far become your reality.

Write your own letter to God:

24TH LETTER

Jireh: You are Enough

Dear Christian,

This particular song by Maverick was on replay: JIREH: "I'll never be more loved than I am right now."

And It got me thinking. Everything we want as believers to see and envy has already been given to us. These dimensions are already present like a woman can house a child without getting pregnant.

We've already been helped, loved, granted grace, glorified, blessed, favoured, etc. However, access to different degrees of this dimension falls on how much capacity we have built in the secret place to properly embody them alongside the attached physical manifestations they come with.

So, a child is trying to reach for a gold chain, and you rebuke him because he doesn't know the value, and it'll go straight to his mouth. But as an adult, you know the worth and how to access it easily.

Your level of Christianity matters in accessing the thematic dimensions of the kingdom. The craziest part, it doesn't come cheap. In this kingdom, we still use trade by barter. Time is the currency we trade for access. The more time, the more access.

Isaiah 43:1-4
But now, this is what the LORD says—
he who created you, Jacob,
he who formed you, Israel:
"Do not fear, for I have redeemed you;
I have summoned you by name; you are mine.
2 When you pass through the waters,
I will be with you;
and when you pass through the rivers,
they will not sweep over you.
When you walk through the fire,
you will not be burned;
the flames will not set you ablaze.
3 For I am the LORD your God,
the Holy One of Israel, your Savior;
I give Egypt for your ransom,
Cush ᵃ and Seba in your stead.
4 Since you are precious and honoured in my sight,
and because I love you,
I will give people in exchange for you,
nations in exchange for your life.

I believe these scriptures are enough to comfort you to last a lifetime and to reassure you that Christ sees you as enough just as he wants him to be enough for you and bask in that understanding.

Write your own letter to God:

25ᵀᴴ LETTER

SELF

Dear Christian

    Worship was ongoing, and different songs were sung, but the Holy Spirit spoke to me through 3. 1. Let every other name fade away 2. You are Jehovah - Prosper Ochimana 3. Come and make my heart your home. It's funny how they came in this order. Now let's link.

    1ˢᵗ song, LABELS [names attached to identify] You label that custard bucket you used to put rice, you open it & it's rice inside and so many other things. We raise holy hands, sing "Let Every Other Name Fade Away," and go back to our friends saying, "I have insecurity issues."

    We want every other name to fade away and only Jesus to be seen, but we're quick to throw the toxic names from people away and make excuses for the toxic labels we place by ourselves: "I don't think I can, I doubt this is for me..." This leads me to song 2

    "You are the mighty man in battle; you are Jehovah." We all see the God that fights our enemies, consuming fire, etc, but fail to see how he fights to save us from us, how we put ourselves in situations against his leading and exploit his faithfulness.

We give him an ultimatum and expect the pain to just varnish, and in his infinite mercies, he saves us from changing; he helps us filter the pain from the challenge itself and its lessons and preserves our sanity. And then song 3: Come and make my heart your HOME

Home: For protection, where you have the liberty to be yourself, where you can relax, where you can rest. When every other name has really faded, he's saved us from ourselves, and we have truly been sold out; He uses us at will & communicates to us with ease. But SELF has to submit.

Write your own letter to God:

26TH LETTER

Jesus As the Light of the World

Dear Christian

Matt 6:22-23a The eye is the light of the body; so if your eye is clear [spiritually perceptive], your whole body will be full of light [benefiting from God's precepts]. But if your eye is bad [spiritually blind], your whole body will be full of darkness [devoid of God's precepts]

And Jesus IS THE LIGHT OF THE WORLD. Through him, the darkness (challenges of this world are filtered). There's so much more to you that you can only see through the light of God, but you need to properly align yourself with him first.

When you lose faith, hope, and trust; When it doesn't make sense; When you stumble and fall, he's there. He's the bigger person, so he has to come through. He's not looking for perfection. Give your life to him, start with your baby steps, and he'll meet you halfway.

"Arise, shine, for YOUR light has come" Isaiah 60:1

What's the usefulness of a torch light when there is light everywhere? And what's the usefulness of a candle when there's a torchlight?

The Bible didn't say "light has come" but was specifically "your."

Specificity of "your light" 1. Understanding 2. Time: Pending when you get 1. Hence, backing up the b part, "the glory of the lord rises upon you" crowns it. But first, you'll have to undergo the process to arise (emerge). So much that you radiate and begin to bask in YOUR LIGHT.

His light is available, but you'd have to use his light to find your light for his light to be more effective.

Write your own letter to God:

27TH LETTER

Tradition

Dear Christian

The Bible didn't record it, but I can imagine the Israelites telling Moses after 430 years, "Our fathers and ancestors served the Egyptians. It is Tradition! We told you to allow us to serve them. They cried to God in Chapter 2. Chapter 14, they were accepting oppression as a trophy.

Exodus 14: 10-12

As Pharaoh approached, the Israelites looked up, and there were the Egyptians, marching after them. They were terrified and cried out to the LORD. **11** They said to Moses, "Was it because there were no graves in Egypt that you brought us to the desert to die? What have you done to us by bringing us out of Egypt? **12** Didn't we say to you in Egypt, 'Leave us alone; let us serve the Egyptians'? It would have been better for us to serve the Egyptians than to die in the desert!"

Isn't it what happens in Sexual Abuse cases? The oppressor, usually the abuser, issues threats and tension when you've come out and because you've kept quiet for so long, you or your parents back out. Indirectly apologizing. They are the same evils, just different forms. The Bible is real.

The pillars of cloud and fire moved to the back when the Egyptians started chasing the Israelites. God's way of saying, "If you want to touch my people, you're gonna have to go through me."

The most humorous part is Pharaoh chasing the Israelites in the middle of the sea. Didn't he see it was strange? Was it his magicians that divided the sea? The audacity to use your enemy's property and you didn't think it would backfire. Safe to say a healthy prayer for God to blind your enemies, please.

Write your own letter to God:

28TH LETTER

Walking in the Light of God

Dear Christian,

While I was praying and washing up, he brought a pictorial view of a covered light. Then Mtt 5:14-16 dropped in my heart: 14 Yea are the world's light. A city that is set on a hill cannot be hidden.

15 Neither do men light a candle, and put it under a bushel, but on a candlestick, and it giveth light unto all in the house. 16 Let your light so shine before men, that they may see your good works, and glorify your Father which is in heaven.

So:

1. I am light. I'm not carrying light. The whole of me is light, and through me, the world is meant to see clearer and better even as I bounce off Christ's light from John 1:9 The true light that gives light to everyone was coming into the world.

2. If a city on a hill cannot be hidden, a bright light shines and cannot be dimmed, so it can't be hidden. 3. The purpose is to see if I turn on my phone torch in the dark. It makes zero sense to sit on the light as this is self-sabotage.

This is why Jesus said men do not light a candle and put it under a bushel. However, that doesn't mean other people can't put a bushel over the light because it'll be foolish to think everyone wants to see when you're seeing or that your light is not affecting people's sight.

What if they want to sleep? Or they have their light, and your light is bringing different rays and making them uncomfortable, and they want only one light to dominate... Whatever their reason, God tells you to arise; your light is here!

There's a way light can be turned on for a long time, and it'll be very hot and still bright. On the flip side, it can grow dim. Since Jesus is the true light, we must go back to seriously beholding Christ, recharging our light so we're too hot for any bushel to be placed on us. So automatically as light, the glory of the lord comes upon us, giving our light backing. So much so that nations/Kings notice the brightness and are drawn to it.

Use this understanding to read the whole of Isaiah 60. All the blessings start with the understanding that you're light in itself, the glory of God you get from beholding Jesus; the true light forever back you. The more you look at him, you become him. By so doing,

Your sun will never set again, and your moon will wane no more; the Lord will be your everlasting light, and your days of sorrow will end. ... To someone out there, the Lord says he's creating new pathways, and this is the first step to walk in them.

Dear Christian, 1. Find the true light, 2. Immerse yourself so much in this light that your light has intense volume. By so doing, you will never grow dim. 3. Walk in this knowledge and enter the pathway God wants to lead you to. 4. Your days of sorrow will end.

Write your own letter to God:

29TH LETTER

Consciousness of the Holy Spirit

Dear Christian

A thread on the consciousness of the Holy Spirit, inspired by the Holy Spirit.

So, it was the last day of #5NOG2021, and the consciousness of the Holy Spirit was being preached. I was tired and began to doze off, then I caught myself and stretched my legs before getting back in, and here's what the Holy Spirit brought to my attention.

If a woman does not get pregnant, she'll never be able to "practically" understand how her womb works. She knows it's there; she can't see it. So, if a woman is pregnant, what does she do? She starts eating for two and is "conscious" that she's carrying life in her.

You know you have the Holy Spirit in you; what are you doing to feed that consciousness? The truth is man is a spirit being that has become too physical, subconsciously making him not align with his spiritual inheritance. What do I mean?

No matter the message they preached in church today, if a man points a gun at someone who was in attendance, he'll probably be afraid. Being conscious of the Holy Spirit daily is intentionality shown through daily fellowship, faith-building, and readiness to be dead and hidden in him.

Paul said, "We're seated in heavenly places." John the Baptist said, "Greater is he that is in me," and Jesus said, "Don't you know ye are gods?" When we are truly conscious, as gods, we become portals, transcending spiritual and physical dimensions and being oracles of God

To be conscious of the Holy Spirit every single day is to fully operate in a spiritual understanding that comes from a Holy Ghost revival of your mind, birthing healing, miracles, and strange spiritual things.

Paul hugged a dead man & he came back to life. It's the same with Elisha's TOMB; Peter's Shadow healed the sick. Dear Christian, these dimensions exist; you're just dwelling so much in the physical and, by so doing, limiting and "under-using" the Holy Spirit.

Write your own letter to God:

30ᵀᴴ LETTER
The Magnificence of God

Dear Christian

Stretch out your palm, and try to fit your full name in one line. You'll find that you can roughly do four people's names on your palm. Here's how the Bible describes God's palms;

Isaiah 49:15b-16a But even if that were possible, I would not forget you! 16. See, I have written your name on the palms of my hands.

Now, God has written your full name on his palm. How big is the palm of God that he has written over 6 BILLION names in it? Now, how big is he? I can't imagine it because it's beyond anything my brain can comprehend. I've never seen anything like it, so I can't compare. I'm pretty sure you can't, too. Even if we found someone with the most tattooed names on their bodies for the Guinness World Record, I doubt we would get 1 billion names.

Point: We truly don't know 0.1 percent of God's magnificence. It is safe to say that our perception of him is flawed. David had to say, "Give me understanding that I might live." So if God is not giving you understanding, you're merely existing. The question thus is: What lenses are you using to view the magnificence of God, and how does this translate to guaranteeing your experience of the fullness of life?

Think deeply about these questions because if answered correctly, your life may take a very different turn, positively, and continue progressing from the understanding you would have gotten.

Write your own letter to God:

31ST LETTER

The Goodness of God

Dear Christian,

Let's talk in-depth about the goodness of God (the core of God's existence)

I was streaming a praise session when the popular song came on "with every breath that I am able, I will sing of the goodness of God," for some reason, it just stayed in my spirit, and I decided to understand better.

The first time we see the word "good" in the Bible was in the creation story. Gen 1:31- "God saw everything that He had made, and behold, it was very good, and He validated it completely." For God himself to validate using the word "good" describes a state of perfection.

His creation was "amazing," "beautiful," "unique," and "special," but the umbrella word the almighty would use to describe everything is that it was "GOOD." This is because this is what he is himself. What do I mean?

James 1:17: "Every good and perfect gift is from above, coming down from the Father of the heavenly lights, with whom there is no change or shifting shadow."

So, if there is a perfect gift, James tells us there are bad and imperfect gifts.

You see, humans have a degree of goodness and badness in them. We are not and cannot be completely good because of the flesh. If we could be, then Paul wouldn't have said to conform and be transformed to Christ's images and likeness.

There would be no need to have the fruit of the spirit because in the fruits is still "goodness." God has no degree of badness in him, and because we're used to saying the word "good," we don't understand it; maybe we never truly have.

Exodus 33-18-20 18 Moses said, "Now show me your glory." 19 And the Lord said, "I will cause all my goodness to pass in front of you, and I will proclaim my name... 20But," he said, "you cannot see my face, for no one may see me and live."

So God was saying, you cannot see my face and live; you cannot see my glory, but I can show you my goodness, which is enough for you as a human. That is the highest degree of divinity you can take, and it suffices.

David also understood this and told us there is more to the goodness of God than we see. In Psalm 23:6, "SURELY, goodness and mercy shall follow me all the days of my life, and I shall dwell in the house of the LORD forever."

David said I'm confident that if I have your goodness and mercy accompanying me, that's all I need to do in life. That provided I dwell in you, your goodness is the spiritual guard, the attribute that comes with your spirit and creates an atmosphere of possibilities...

Where I know you're with me all the days of my life.

How do I know this is what David was saying? 2 Kings 5:26a But Elisha said, "Was not my spirit with you when the man got down from his chariot to meet you?

If the spirit of a man can follow another man, how much more an attribute of God himself that he can send as an atmosphere as we see he did for Moses, confirmed by David, who further shows us in his psalms that truly the goodness of God is an experience.

Psalm 27:13: "I remain confident of this: I will see the goodness of the LORD in the land of the living." This means that there are indices that physically show that God's goodness is truly following you. This is why he says again in

Psalm 65:11: "You crown the year with Your goodness, And Your paths drip with abundance." And no, we're not leaving Paul out because Paul told us to in

Rom 8:28: "And we know that all things work together for good to those who love God, to those who are the called according to His purpose." This is why we understand that, whether bad or even good things, eventually, they'll work FOR US!

Because we are of God, walking in his purpose, and if his love, word, help, grace, favour, etc., is rooted in his goodness, then we can rest easy. This is how simple the word is when the Holy Spirit brings light.

Sometimes, as Christians, we think the seemingly heavy spiritual activities count/matter. It is because God is good that he keeps his word. It is because God is good, and his goodness is so perfect that he can be loved! (1 John 4:16)

Today, as I have received light, I bring it to you. When you say "God is Good," know you're prophesying. You're saying God has NO degree of badness. His divinity doesn't permit it. His goodness is the core of his existence and being as God.

So even in that situation that looks bad, GOD IS GOOD! The goodness of God overrides, overturns, and programs the situation. HIS GOODNESS IS ENOUGH! Cliché but Gold: "God is good, ALL the time and ALL the time, GOD IS GOOD."

Write your own letter to God:

32ND LETTER
Love Changes (Context; Romantic Love-Marriage)

Dear Christian,

I was conversing yesterday when I said, "committed to loving your partner daily." And today, more light came, and I'll share as led. So, while worshiping, sometimes the Holy Spirit teaches me, and this time, he said, "Love Changes!"

As Christians, The Bible says, "submit yourselves to God..." How do we submit? By living in obedience to his word. How do we do this? By DAILY surrendering. Surrendering on its own is tough, so we don't think of how we will surrender futuristically.

So we surrender our will and submit to his DAILY! The HS said, how do we know we submit to Christ through the written word? Then he said likewise, your partner. Their word (what they like, want, how they like you to do certain things) SUBJECTED TO THE SCRIPTURES,

It is how you submit in love for BOTH parties. John 12:24: "Very truly I tell you, unless a kernel of wheat falls to the ground and dies, it remains only a single seed. But if it dies, it produces many seeds."

So, In our love walk with Christ, we kill our flesh daily to pick up the life Christ wants for us for our profit. Likewise, in marriage, both parties, already being Christians and submitting to God, then further kill their selfish desires, seeing that they're already one.

I subdue my flesh to submit to the words of my partner under Christ, and he does that for me, too. We eventually have the type of man I need, and he gets the type of woman he needs. Provided it's in Christ, ultimately, this makes us grow better for each other.

So yes, as the scriptures stand as our law for a living, our partner's needs should come right after. Is this tough? I promise you that my coconut head has not accepted what I'm typing. However, it is for the good of both parties.

The more I advance in learning, the more I understand why the Bible is said to be equally yoked. Love is something! Intoxicating, flirting, ephemeral, subjective, call it whatever, and sometimes, due to our varied definitions, some people have ended up with the wrong love.

If you're not a Christian, this post is not for you. In the same way, if you're unequally yoked, your partner may not even understand or relate to everything this thread has communicated, which may or may not be frustrating given their current love situation.

Submitted to Christ under a beautiful and intentional love exchange "counts" for an amazing life in our world. May we give this kind of love and receive it, too. Amen!

Write your own letter to God:

33ʳᵈ LETTER
Help from God

Dear Christian,

Let's look at the Widow Elisha Helped.
It is a story of Help, the Holy Spirit, Perspective on life, and Availability for God.
It may just be the TGIF you need.
2 Kings 4:1-7

A Thread
When the instruction was given, the woman didn't understand the miracle most of us can relate to. God never tells you WHY. He tells you WHAT initially, then you find out HOW you'll do it, and in this obedience, you see WHY in the evident miracle.

So faith has to be applied first, but let's look at how the woman followed the instructions. "Don't borrow a few." I think she had a small mind or a non-resilient attitude to life.

4. Then go inside and shut the door behind you and your sons. Pour oil into all the jars, and as each is filled, put it to one side." 5. She left him and shut the door behind her and her sons. They brought the jars to her, and she kept pouring.

6. When all the jars were full, she told her son, "Bring me another one." But he replied, "There is not a jar left." Then,

the oil stopped flowing. ... An important thing to note here is that the oil didn't stop when she stopped pouring, but when the son said, "There is no jar."

7. She told the man of God, and he said, "Go, sell the oil, and pay your debts. You and your sons can live on what is left." ... So, the big picture was to have an oil business. The miracle was God himself giving her the capital she needed.

But we can't judge the woman; we can only learn from her. We can also know it's not everything a Man of God or even God will tell us; in the process, we eventually find out. Albeit, if we approach life from a conquering standpoint, we may see far.

Lastly, in the New Testament, we are the vessels! We are given prophetic instructions occasionally, and God's help has been supplied. As vessels, we are the only channels for the oil to pass through. Oil is the Holy Spirit.

Thus, how much space inside us have we made available for the Holy Spirit to fill up? Here, the more space we make available for him to occupy, the more jars he's filling for us to sell to the nations.

The less space we give him, the more the jar finishes. Now, the idea is that, as he fills us up, we sell to the world and empty more spaces in our lives, surrendering it to him to use. So, it becomes a lineup of jars. Filled and exported, the empty jar returns in line.

We empty more spaces, make room for more jars, and just like that, in our social, physical, career, and every aspect, we are being filled up and selling the jars and returning for more filling. Thus, continuously experiencing the miracle of God's help and sufficiency, which is ENOUGH!

This woman could have easily become a big businesswoman and oil tycoon. God himself gave you capital. But well, May God help us all. Okay, Bye

Write your own letter to God:

34TH LETTER

Brokeness in Christ

Dear Christian,

Let's look at the Samarian woman through the lens of her love life.

This thread may break something in you but give you peace at the same time.

John 4: 16-42.

1. What made her to continue remarrying? 2. What was she looking for in her marriages? 3. Why didn't she give up on marriage even after five men? 4. Why was she living with a man she wasn't married to, knowing he wasn't her husband?

She was just a woman who wanted to get it right but didn't know how to. She is a very genuine woman at her core because she could even have easily assumed the man she was living with into a husband role when Jesus asked to save face, but she told this stranger,

"I don't have a husband." I will not ignore the saying that when everybody has a problem with you, you may be the problem. So, In this case, she was most likely the problem as genuine as she was. Sometimes, we may be genuine, and yes, God sees our hearts, but it may not be enough.

27. "Just then, his disciples came back. They were shocked to find him talking to a woman, but none of them had the nerve to ask, "What do you want with her?" "Why are you talking to her?" So Jesus was alone with this woman. Damning all gender/ societal consequences and question

Mind you, this was the longest conversation Jesus ever had in the Bible with someone alone. What was it about this woman that Jesus was investing so much? He saw THE STATE OF HER HEART. He knew this woman just wanted to get it right even after being told...

She wasn't enough with five husbands & another man, but didn't give up. He knew that if he reached her, he could reach the whole city because of her heart, and he wasn't wrong. In v 26, Jesus told her he was the Messiah before the disciples came. Watch the next thing she did

28. The woman left her water jar beside the well and RAN back to the village, telling everyone. 29"Come see a man who told me everything I ever did! Could he possibly be the Messiah?" It is important to note that Jesus did not tell the woman to spread the news.

As a matter of fact, he didn't even do any miracle for her at that point. I can imagine the woman thinking, "he knew everything about me. He didn't judge me..." and just by that gesture, she RAN to tell everybody, come and see this man whose actions have warmed my heart.

I cannot see this alone. As a result of that action, a whole city believed! 39. Many Samaritans from the village believed in Jesus because the woman had said, "He told me everything I ever did!" To be genuine is to be sincere, real, and honest.

Summarily, Jesus needs genuinely broken people who have a big mouths! A testifying tongue that won't hold back even the "littlest" things he does for them but spreads it so that others may come to the true light.

So, this new week and beyond, there are two things you need to check. 1. How much of a genuine person are you? Can Christ trust you not to lie to him, starting with telling yourself the truth? 2. How broken in Christ are you? ... May we do better. May we be better!

Write your own letter to God:

35TH LETTER
The Christian Journey
[A charge]

Dear Christian,

The Christian journey is difficult, and humans make it even more challenging.

I got into a little social media brawl with someone I felt wanted to misunderstand or spite me purposely. So my aunt, the only person who gets through to me, quickly saw a response I made to someone and told me, "You could have taken the high road, Lois."

I told her, but I can feel this person's vileness and bitterness. You make a Twitter thread that people don't want to read. They want to take the part they use to tail and spew to carpet you. Forgetting that not only do they have the monopoly of a rash speech.

Sometimes, you must tell these people they can't succeed in bullying you. Then she made me understand that this person may have been genuinely bitter, but what if you reached out to them more lovingly and won them over for Jesus? As annoying as that sounded. She was right.

And this is how God molds and changes us. Little by little, bit by bit, pulling out the layers of our flesh. I was even giving myself credit that if it were before, I would have replied in the same measure, but Jesus is changing me, and my aunt came to say, you can do more.

Either way, God is changing us, working on our hearts, and while it's beautiful to see, know that Christians are still humans; all of us are not on the same growth spectrum, and very important is that APPROACH IS KEY.

I'm stress-free and like to radiate only positivity; I protect my joy and heart from toxicity. I can smell love like I smell bad energy from a distance. We don't all have it together; not everyone will be like us. People should also be kind in their speech to avoid appearing provocative.

Col 4:6

Let your conversation be always gracious, seasoned with salt, so you may know how to answer everyone.

So, this is my reminder to make your speech filled with grace and honour. It's not easy, but we will allow God to work with our hearts and humanity through us.

Write your own letter to God:

36TH LETTER

Be it unto you.

Dear Christian

Mtt 9:27-30a 27. And when Jesus departed thence, two blind men followed him, crying and saying, Thou Son of David, have mercy on us. 28. When he came into the house, the blind men came to him: and Jesus saith unto them, Believe ye that I can do this?

They said unto him, Yea, Lord. 29. Then touched their eyes, saying, According to your faith be it unto you. 30 And their eyes were opened;" … There was a faith process to the healing of the blind men. A cry for mercy, following Jesus (in this case, not giving up.)

They were blind, so this was a reach. They didn't just sit by the roadside crying. They wanted a miracle. After that, Jesus still asked them, do you believe I can do it? Wasn't their faith enough already? He had to probe them still further. Even after saying yes,

Their sight was not restored. He touched their eyes and said, "Be it unto you according to your faith." This was a conditional miracle. The condition is the degree of their "submittedness" to the word of God. This was when they regained their sight.

Jesus said: Be it into you according to your faith. Mary said: Be it into me according to your word. "Faith comes by hearing & hearing the word." In essence, Jesus was saying Be it unto you according to the faith you have built from the rooted word in you and your submission to it.

Thus, everything has been given to the believer to dominate the earth. How much of God's word in promises and instructions that lead to these promises DO YOU KNOW, BELIEVE, and ACT ON? Some of us are in the blind men situation, but maybe we're playing the victim.

"God, can't you see? What else do you want me to do? I'm tired; I've tried!" That's fair enough, but maybe we need to adopt the strength of the blind men. Not because God is wicked but because it takes faith to PLEASE HIM.

The irony of everything still ends up being that in pleasing God, our transformation is his utmost goal. That we are furnished, rooted, and able to stand firm. That we transcend from baby believers to withstand the wiles of the devil. That we are trained and pruned as ambassadors.

It is through this tough training that we cannot just stand but stand FIRM. This is the aim of the faith process, and in this, the father is pleased that he has raised a fierce witness and tough soldier that he can trust to the nations. Tested and tried!

Like 1:37, The angel said for with God, nothing is impossible. Then Mary answered, Be it unto me according to your word. So the prayer is that we trust the word enough and the one who spoke it to submit to whatever it does in us. Amen and Amen!!!

Write your own letter to God:

37TH LETTER
Permission/consent

Dear Christian

The Holy Spirit said to tell you...

The more an individual frequents a building, the more you might think he has affiliations with the owner or, in some cases, think he's the owner himself. The reason is that he's always permitted to enter by the gateman or his keys.

So, say your parents own your house, but they know some of your friends due to frequent visits. For the friends they don't approve of when they're not around, you permit them personally. Again, they would usually knock before coming into your room.

You've been bought with a price, but like your parents knock on your door, he hits on your heart. You may be tired, frustrated, or depressed for whatever reason. It could be wrong choices, terrible decisions, or things you can't explain or understand.

Often, it's because you've opened your doors too wide and permitted things and people into your life. Knowingly and unknowingly, you forget or are even ignorant that it's your space, you're in charge, you've got the keys, and you can choose who you want to permit.

However, the catch is that your physical liberties don't function in spiritual jurisdictions. The world is both physical & spiritual. Governed by the spiritual, you must have a strong spiritual force in your corner to win on both ends. The more reason you need to let him in

Once you do, he takes charge, shuts the door to irrelevant visitors of your destiny, and directs you on how to run your life better. He wants to help you, but he needs your permission. Give/re-dedicate your life to Christ.

Write your own letter to God:

38TH LETTER

Lukewarm Christianity

Dear Christian,

We raise our hands in worship, singing songs like "Feel me up till I overflow, I wanna run over" or "We thirst for you In a dry and barren land."...

While these are amazing songs, we may sing them from an incomplete understanding point.

Jesus to the woman at Jacob's well: John 4:13 Jesus replied, "Anyone who drinks this water will soon become thirsty again. 14 But those who drink the water I give will never be thirsty again. It becomes a fresh, bubbling spring within them, giving them eternal life."

The truth is that several Christians want that balance, including me. I don't want it to be too cold or hot—just room temperature. But room temperature can be classified as cold because it doesn't tilt toward hot.

So here's what the Holy Spirit said: mixing the cup of the flesh and the cup of the spirit is impossible. If the flesh is contending with the spirit, how can the living water fill you up and overflow? You'll never get filled because the flesh will keep diluting it.

The woman at Jacobs Well said: "How can you offer better water than he and his sons and his animals enjoyed?" From the flesh standpoint, you'll never understand how filling the living water is. Oh, here's the best part: overflowing water doesn't have a specific direction.

So when he fills you up and your cup overflows, there are no boundaries in outreach, blessing, and sacrifice. He flows through you from within. ABUNDANTLY! Let him fill you up.

Write your own letter to God:

39TH LETTER

The Samarian Woman

Dear Christian,

Let's look at the Samarian woman through the lens of her love life.

John 4:16-17- 16: "Go and get your husband," Jesus told her. 17"I don't have a husband," the woman replied. Jesus said, "You're right! You don't have a husband."

Before this, a conversation led to a Samarian woman begging for the living water. Jesus didn't give her the water she was asking for but wanted to test her by asking her to get her husband. Of which she replied to him truthfully.

18. you have had five husbands and aren't even married to the man you're living with now. You certainly spoke the truth!" Imagine a situation where the woman, ignorant that Jesus already knew her, lied to him. but let's focus on her love life to understand her.

1. What made her to continue remarrying? 2. What was she looking for in her marriages? 3. Why didn't she give up on marriage even after five men? 4. Why was she living with a man she wasn't married to, knowing he wasn't her husband?

I think she was just a woman who wanted to get it right but didn't know how to. She is a very genuine woman at her core because she could even have easily assumed the man she was living with into a husband role when Jesus asked to save face, but she told this stranger,

"I don't have a husband." I will not ignore the saying that when everybody has a problem with you, you may be the problem. So, In this case, she was most likely the problem as genuine as she was. Sometimes, we may be genuine, and yes, God sees our hearts, but it may not be enough.

27. "Just then, his disciples came back. They were shocked to find him talking to a woman, but none of them had the nerve to ask, "What do you want with her?" "Why are you talking to her?" So Jesus was alone with this woman. Damning all gender/ societal consequences and questions

Mind you, this was the longest conversation Jesus ever had in the Bible with someone alone. What was it about this woman that Jesus was investing so much? He saw THE STATE OF HER HEART. He knew this woman just wanted to get it right even after being told…

she wasn't enough with five husbands & another man, but didn't give up. He knew that if he reached her, he could reach the whole city because of her heart, and he wasn't wrong. In v 26, Jesus told her he was the Messiah before the disciples came. Watch the next thing she did

28. The woman left her water jar beside the well and RAN back to the village, telling everyone. 29"Come see a man who told me everything I ever did! Could he possibly be the Messiah?" It is important to note that Jesus did not tell the woman to spread the news.

As a matter of fact, he didn't even do any miracle for her at that point. I can imagine the woman thinking, "he knew everything about me; he didn't judge me…" and just by that gesture, she RAN to tell everybody, come and see this man whose actions have warmed my heart.

I cannot see this alone. As a result of that action, a whole city believed! 39. Many Samaritans from the village believed in Jesus because the woman had said, "He told me everything I ever did!" To be genuine is to be sincere, real, and honest.

Summarily, Jesus needs genuinely broken people who have a big mouths! A testifying tongue that won't hold back even the "littlest" things he does for them but spreads it so that others may come to the true light.

So, this new week and beyond, there are two things you need to check. 1. How much of a genuine person are you? Can Christ trust you not to lie to him, starting with telling yourself the truth? 2. How broken in Christ are you? ... May we do better. May we be better!

Write your own letter to God:

40TH LETTER
Expressing Vulnerability

Dear Christian,

This is my last letter to you on this issue, and I hope my journey has blessed you even as Christ is still working in me.

As you chase life and things get overwhelming,

As you strive to find the balance between professing your faith and building a haven to keep your doubts away, never forget this line is blurry.

Yes, out of the haven is the need to voice out your vulnerability, but inside the haven is the fear of unwanted projected insecurities, Knowingly and unknowingly, from people who genuinely care about you and are even a part of your support system.

You must realize that you cannot wait till all is okay with you to act and take steps in life. Thus, it would help if you found a balance that draws strength in the well-being and growth of people and seeks to encourage them.

By so doing, you are reminded, no matter how easy it is to forget, that True sanity will always precede the rule that states, "One day at a time with Jesus". Matthew 11:28-30 says: "Come to me, all you who are weary and burdened, and I will give you rest. Take my yoke upon you and learn from me, for I am gentle and humble in heart, and you will find rest for your souls. For my yoke is easy and my burden is light."

It's not been an easy walk. Never has been. But you've been walking it all the same. Keep moving; don't give up. It only gets better.

Till I see you again...

Dear Christian,

I hope you have enjoyed reading my letters that have stemmed from my personal walk with Christ. As you journey on your own, the key thing to remember is that- it is "Your" walk with Christ. It goes beyond what your church says and what spiritual leaders have to say. Yes, they will be very vital and instrumental in your journey, however, you have to own your relationship with Christ and make it what you want it to be. This is because Christianity is a personal race and the onus is on you to work out your salvation. Whether you have an amazing life with Christ or a Luke warm relationship, rises and falls on you. It is your sole responsibility to read your bible, pray and talk to the Holy Spirit, asking him for guidance. He is already there waiting for you. If you draw near to him, he will draw near to you.

Repetition is for emphasis they say, so I'll repeat; Christianity, more than a religion, is a relationship and like any other relationship that you cultivate with two willing partners, you will most definitely reap the good fruits.

With Love,
Lois Tarikabor

Write your own letter to God:

www.ingramcontent.com/pod-product-compliance
Lightning Source LLC
LaVergne TN
LVHW041639060526
838200LV00040B/1631